The Costume Contest

Carnival Luck

Barbara Hoskins

OXFORD
UNIVERSITY PRESS

Oxford University Press
198 Madison Avenue, New York, NY 10016, USA
Great Clarendon Street, Oxford OX2 6DP, England

Oxford New York
Auckland Bangkok Buenos Aires Cape Town Chennai
Dar es Salaam Delhi Hong Kong Istanbul Karachi Kolkata
Kuala Lumpur Madrid Melbourne Mexico City Mumbai Nairobi
São Paulo Shanghai Singapore Taipei Tokyo Toronto

with an associated company in Berlin

OXFORD is a trademark of Oxford University Press.

ISBN 0-19-436466-6

Editorial Manager: Shelagh Speers
Senior Editor: Sherri Arbogast
Editor: Lynne Robertson
Assistant Editor: Christine Hartzler
Production Editor: Mark Steven Long
Elementary Design Manager: Doris Chen Pinzon
Designer: Natacha Menar
Senior Art Buyer: Patricia Marx
Art Buyer: Elizabeth Blomster

Printing (last digit): 10 9 8 7 6 5 4

Printed in Hong Kong.

Illustrations by Sally Springer (Griffith)
Other illustrations by Jim Talbot

Cover design by Doris Chen Pinzon/Natacha Menar
Cover illustration by Sally Springer (Griffith)

For Taka and Miku.

The Costume Contest

"Tomorrow is the school costume contest,"
says Wendy.
"Do you have a costume?" asks Amy.
"Yes, I do," says Wendy. "It's a secret."
"I don't have a costume," says Amy. "I don't
have any ideas."

| costume | costume contest | secret | ideas |

"Hi, Ben," says Wendy. "Do you have a costume?"
"Yes," says Ben. "I'm making it today."
"What is it?" asks Amy.
"Sorry, I can't tell," says Ben. "It's a secret."

"What's he making?" asks Amy. "Let's follow him!"
"OK!" says Wendy.

follow

"Ben's going into that restaurant," says Wendy.
"He can't buy a costume in a restaurant,"
says Amy.

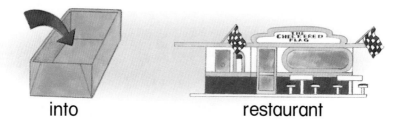

into   restaurant

"Here he comes," says Amy. "Hide!"
"Ben has some paper plates," says Wendy.
"What can he make with those?" asks Amy.

hide   paper plates

"Look!" says Amy. "Ben's buying some green and gray paint."
"Is he making a monster costume?" asks Wendy.

monster costume

"Following Ben is fun!" says Amy.
"Yeah. We're good detectives!" says Wendy.
"But what's Ben's costume?" asks Amy.

Yeah = Yes

detectives

"He's putting everything into a box," says Wendy.
"That's a big box!" says Amy.
"Is he making a robot costume?" asks Wendy.

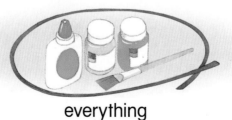

everything

"Let's go home," says Amy. "I can make my costume now. I have an idea."

"What is it?" asks Wendy.

"It's a secret," says Amy.

"Okay," says Wendy. "See you tomorrow!"

Today is the costume contest.
The children are in the gym.
"Amy!" says Wendy. "You're a detective!"
"That's right!" says Amy.
"That's a great costume," says Wendy.

That's right! = Yes!

"I like your costume, too," says Amy.
"Thanks," says Wendy. "Do you want a cookie?"
"Thank you," says Amy. "Where's Ben?"
"I don't know," says Wendy. "But there's David."

"Wow!" says Amy. "David's a camera!"

"A cook and a detective!" says David. "Nice costumes."

"Thanks," says Wendy. "I like your costume, too."

"Where's Ben?" asks Amy.

"You're the detective," says David. "You tell me!"

camera

"Here he is!" says Wendy.

"Hi!" says Ben.

"You're a race car and a driver!" says Amy.

"Great idea!"

"Hey!" says David. "Let's take a picture!"

race car

driver

Great idea!

take a picture

Exercises

A. Match the children to their costumes.

1. Wendy   ———   a. a detective

2. Ben   ———   b. a camera

3. Amy   ———   c. a cook

4. David   ———   d. a race car and a driver

B. Yes or no?

1. Amy and Wendy follow Ben. ☐ Yes ☐ No

2. Wendy makes a monster costume. ☐ Yes ☐ No

3. Ben makes a robot costume. ☐ Yes ☐ No

4. Amy likes Ben's costume. ☐ Yes ☐ No

C. Answer the questions.

1. Where does Ben get paper plates?

2. What color paint does Ben buy?

3. What is David's costume?

4. Where is the costume contest?

D. What about you?

Whose costume do you like?

Carnival Luck

David and Amy were at the carnival.

"Any luck?" asked Amy.

"No," said David. "I never win these games."

carnival

luck

win

"Try again," said Amy.
"Okay," said David. David tossed the coin.

"You won!" said Amy.
"Wow! This is my lucky day!" said David.

win → won

try   try again   tossed   lucky day

"Which dog do you want?" asked the man.

"I don't know," said David. "Which one do you like, Amy?"

"I like the blue one," said Amy.

"I want the big blue dog," said David.

man

David gave his prize to Amy.

"Here, Amy," he said. "You can have the dog."

"Thank you!" said Amy. "It's cute!"

prize   cute

Wendy was at the ring toss.
"Any luck?" asked Amy.
"No, I can't win," said Wendy.

ring toss

"Try again," said David.
"Oh, okay," said Wendy.
Wendy tossed the rings.

"Look!" said Wendy. "I won the camera!"
"You're lucky!" said David.

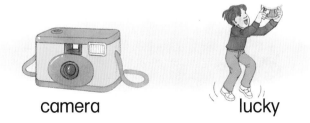

camera   lucky

"Let me try," said Amy.
Amy tossed the rings. She won a model.
"You're lucky, too!" said Wendy.

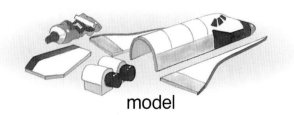

model

"I want a camera," said David.
David tossed the rings. He won a pink panda.
"I won!" said David.
"It's cute," said Amy.

panda

"I like your panda," said Wendy. "Can we trade?"
"Sure," said David. "Thanks! It *is* my lucky day!"

trade

Sure = Yes

They saw Ben at the dart throw.
"Any luck?" asked Wendy.
"No, I can't pop the yellow balloon," said Ben. "I want those tickets."

dart throw   pop   tickets

"Come on! Try again," said David.
"You can do it!" said Amy.
"Okay," said Ben.

Ben threw his last dart. He popped the yellow balloon.

throw → threw   pop → popped

"Here are your tickets," said the woman.
"You did it!" said Amy.
"You won the tickets!" said David.

woman

our

"This is our lucky day!" said Ben. "Let's all go on the roller coaster!"

Exercises

A. Yes or no?

1. David gave the blue dog to Ben. ☐ Yes ☐ No

2. The children are playing darts. ☐ Yes ☐ No

3. Ben popped the yellow balloon. ☐ Yes ☐ No

4. The children went on the roller ☐ Yes ☐ No
   coaster.

B. Put the sentences in order.

_____ David won the blue dog.

_____ Ben won the tickets.

_____ Wendy won the camera.

_____ Amy won the model.

_____ The children went on the roller coaster.

C. Answer the questions.

1. Where are the children?

2. Who won the blue dog?

3. Who won the camera?

4. What did Ben win?

D. What about you?

Which prize do you like?